A GIFT FOR:

_____

FROM:

_____

DR. EMERSON EGGERICHS

Love AND RESPECT

FOR A LIFETIME

THOMAS NELSON
Since 1798

NASHVILLE   DALLAS   MEXICO CITY   RIO DE JANEIRO   BEIJING

Author is represented by the literary agency of Alive Communications, Inc., 7680 Goddard Street, Suite 200, Colorado Springs, CO 80920, www.alivecommunications.com.

Published in Nashville, Tennessee, by Thomas Nelson. Thomas Nelson is a registered trademark of Thomas Nelson, Inc.

Thomas Nelson, Inc. titles may be purchased in bulk for educational, business, fundraising, or sales promotional use. For information, please e-mail *SpecialMarkets@ThomasNelson.com*.

Compiled by Terri Gibbs

Project Manager: Lisa Stilwell

ISBN: 978-1-4041-8940-9

Printed and bound in China

10 11 12 13 14 [RRD] 5 4 3 2 1

www.thomasnelson.com

CONTENTS

INTRODUCTION

Ironically, there are more books being published on marriage today than ever before. There are books on marital communication, money management, sex, etc. There are even books on how to become a better husband (or wife) in thirty days! But with all our knowledge, the craziness and conflict continues. And it doesn't seem to matter if the couples are Christians or unbelievers. Why? I have concluded that those of us in the church, who believe we have the Truth, are not using the whole truth. A crucial part of God's Word has been completely ignored or perhaps simply gone unnoticed when it has been there all the time right under our noses!

Many Christian spouses know Ephesians 5:33 and can at least paraphrase it. The apostle Paul tells husbands to love their wives as much as they love themselves, and wives are to respect their husbands. But is anyone really listening? Perhaps the first step to better communication between husband and wife is to hear what God's Word clearly says, because living out Ephesians 5:33 is the key to blending together as one to reflect the very image of God.

This book will show you the power of unconditional love and unconditional respect. As you and your spouse use these powerful tools, you can save a struggling marriage from the divorce court or a "ho-hum" marriage from boredom and concealed bitterness. If you have a good marriage, you can make it even better.

—EMERSON EGGERICHS

THE WISDOM OF LOVE AND RESPECT

A woman needs love like she needs
air to breathe. A man need respect
like he needs air to breathe.

The first question some folks ask is "Don't women need respect and men need love?" Absolutely. We all need love and respect equally. However, Ephesians 5:33 says that a husband must love his wife and a wife must respect her husband. Apparently there is a felt need in a wife for love and, in a husband, for respect. Assuming this to be true but wanting to validate it, we asked seven thousand people this question: *During a conflict with your spouse, do you feel unloved or disrespected*? Eighty-three percent of the men said they feel disrespected, and 72 percent of the women feel unloved.

When your spouse's spirit deflates during a conflict, your wife is feeling unloved and your husband is feeling disrespected. Not always, but frequently. When a husband chooses to do or say something loving—and that includes saying, "I am sorry for coming across in an unloving way"—he energizes his wife. When a wife decides to express herself respectfully—and that includes apologizing for her disrespectful attitude—she energizes her husband.

OH, THAT COUPLES WOULD DISCOVER *the* POWER OF LOVE *and* RESPECT!

LOVE *and* RESPECT ARE LIKE OXYGEN TO *a* SUFFOCATING PERSON, *and* THIS IS ONE REASON WHY GOD COMMANDS *a* HUSBAND TO LOVE AND *a* WIFE TO RESPECT!

What do you want for your marriage? Do you want some peace? Do you want to feel close to each other? Do you want to feel valued by each other? Do you want to experience marriage the way God intended? Then why not try some Love and Respect? It will change the way you talk to, think about, and treat each other. It will change your marriage!

Here is the secret to marriage that every couple seeks, and yet few couples ever find . . .

Unconditional respect is as powerful for him as unconditional love is for her.

It's the secret that will help you achieve a brand new level of intimacy.

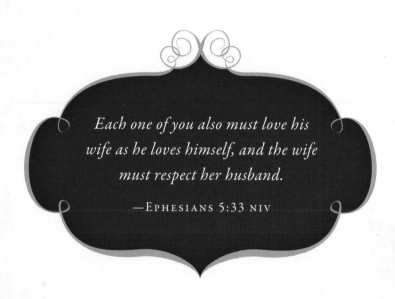

Each one of you also must love his wife as he loves himself, and the wife must respect her husband.

—Ephesians 5:33 NIV

You're the only person in the world who can meet your spouse's deepest need for love and respect in marriage. After all, you alone are married to your spouse!

When you touch your spouse's deepest need, something good almost always happens. The key to energizing your spouse is meeting your spouse's heartfelt desire.

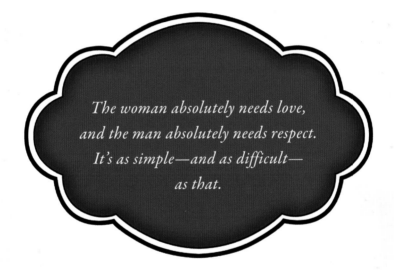

*The woman absolutely needs love,
and the man absolutely needs respect.
It's as simple—and as difficult—
as that.*

Respect is a man's deepest value. I have had numerous men tell me, "I would rather live with a wife who respected me but did not love me than live with a wife who loved me but did not respect me."

These men are not saying that they are indifferent to love. They know they need love, but they need to feel respected even more than to feel loved.

Your husband needs you to love him,
but he also needs you to like him
as a friend.

When you come home after you have been apart, the first few moments of reconnecting will set the tone for the rest of the evening.

When his wife shows him unconditional respect, in most cases a husband will feel like a prince and be motivated to show her the kind of unconditional love she desires. She is not a doormat or a slave. She is a princess who is loved and, by the way, respected also.

She wants him to BRING FLOWERS. He would rather FIX THE FAUCET. He needs to see that she wants flowers. She needs to see and appreciate that he wants to fix the sink.

A WIFE HAS ONE DRIVING NEED—
TO FEEL LOVED. WHEN THAT NEED
is MET, SHE *is* HAPPY.

A HUSBAND HAS ONE DRIVING
NEED—TO FEEL RESPECTED.
WHEN THAT NEED *is* MET, HE *is* HAPPY.

WHEN EITHER *of* THESE NEEDS
ISN'T MET, THINGS GET CRAZY
WITH CONFLICT.

AS *D*IFFERENT AS PINK IS FROM BLUE

Together, you and your mate
reflect the image of God on earth.

I remind couples of Genesis 1:27 that "male and female He created them" and that we are as different as pink is from blue. I also remind couples that Genesis 1:27 states, "God created man in His own image, in the image of God He created them." In other words, together in marriage, a blue husband and a pink wife reflect the image of God. Interestingly, when we blend pink and blue, they form the color purple, the color of royalty, the color of God.

IN OTHER WORDS, TOGETHER *a* WIFE AND *a* HUSBAND REFLECT *the* ROYAL IMAGE *of* GOD ON EARTH. GOD IS NOT PINK. GOD IS NOT BLUE. GOD *is* PURPLE. WHEN TWO BECOME ONE, THEY HAVE THE POTENTIAL *of* DISPLAYING GOD'S ATTRIBUTES AND CHARACTER.

Amazingly, many married people have been blown away by this imagery. "The first thing that revolutionized my thinking and paradigm," says one wife, "was that the issues are not so much a 'Jim and Pam' thing as a male-female thing. That realization caused me to weep. It freed me so much to know that our differences of pink and blue will become purple as Jim and I surrender and depend upon the Lord as we work through our issues."

God created man in
His own image . . . male and female
He created them.

—GENESIS 1:27

Women look at the world through pink sunglasses, while men look at that same world through blue sunglasses— and, believe me, they do not necessarily see the same thing!

The differences between men and women were established from the beginning. Women tend to be relationship oriented, and the family is their primary place for relationships. The deepest question you can ask a woman—a question she asks herself quite often—is "Are you loved?"

Men, however, tend to be achievement-oriented, and their "field" is the primary place for achievement. The deepest question you can ask a man—a question that he asks himself quite often—is "Are you respected?" No wonder, then, that in a marriage the wife wants her husband to be more loving, and the husband wants his wife to be more respectful.

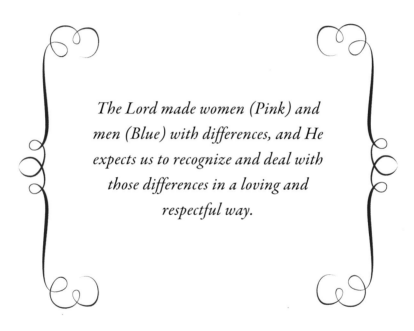

The Lord made women (Pink) and men (Blue) with differences, and He expects us to recognize and deal with those differences in a loving and respectful way.

Why is communication between husbands and wives such a problem? It goes back to the fact that we send each other messages in "code," based on gender, even though we don't intend to. What I say is not what you hear, and what you think you heard is not what I meant at all.

Men and women both need love and both need respect. But the cry from a woman's deepest soul is to be loved and the cry from a man's deepest soul is to be respected.

Couples practicing Love and Respect learn that their communication styles are markedly different. In order to understand these differences, they need to realize that they send each other messages in code and they must learn how to decode each other.

For example, one wife wrote to share this decoding experience with us:

[My husband and I] were traveling in the car on our way to a movie. He was quiet and smiling smugly. I said, "What are you thinking?" He replied, "I was just thinking how critical you are."

My natural instinct was . . . how dare him! But I thought, *This is a good-willed man. Maybe he means something else.* So I asked, "What does that mean, that I'm critical?" He replied, "I mean our family couldn't exist without you. You are so critical to us."

> *It is crucial for husband and wife to see that neither one is wrong, but that both of them are very different—in body function, outlook, and perspective.*

Pink and blue perceptions not only affect seeing; they affect hearing as well. Women hear with pink hearing aids and men hear with blue hearing aids. Even more important to understand as you and your spouse seek to gain better communication, you can hear the very same words, but each of you will hear different messages.

Let's see how this plays out at home as a couple is getting dressed to start the day:

She says, "I have nothing to wear."
(She means, she has nothing *new*.)

He says, "I have nothing to wear."
(He means, he has nothing *clean*.)

Research and experience prove that men and women see and hear differently. Recognizing these differences and adjusting to them is absolutely necessary for reaching mutual understanding and better communication.

In one national study, four hundred men were given a choice between going through two different negative experiences. If they were forced to choose one of the following, which would they prefer to endure?

a) to be left alone and unloved in the world

b) to feel inadequate and disrespected by everyone

Seventy-four percent of these men said that if they were forced to choose, they would prefer being alone and unloved in the world.

Survey performed by Decision Analysts, Inc. and tabulated by Analytic Focus for Shaunti Feldhahn, For Women Only.)

Every man does what he does for the
admiration of one woman.

—ANONYMOUS

When a wife feels unloved, it can be such a shock to her heart that she is oblivious to her disrespectful reactions toward her husband, though any man watching could see it plainly.

When a husband feels disrespected, it can provoke him so quickly he doesn't see his unloving reaction, which would be obvious to any woman. Words of wisdom for all husbands and wives are these:

WE EASILY SEE WHAT *is* DONE TO US BEFORE WE SEE WHAT WE ARE DOING *to* OUR MATE.

God's way of communicating in marriage is to talk with words of unconditional love and respect.

That's why the one secret to speaking your mate's language is to understand that unconditional respect is as powerful to him as unconditional love is to her.

Your spouse can have a need you
don't have and that's okay.

SHE *N*EEDS LOVE

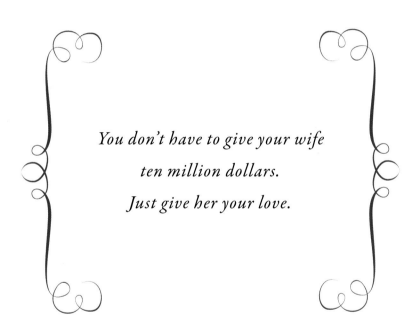

You don't have to give your wife
ten million dollars.
Just give her your love.

"Over the years," says one husband, "my wife dealt with her insecurities through behavior I described as 'controlling.' Each time she engaged in this behavior, I reacted by withdrawing physically and emotionally. For years I complained about her controlling behavior, but the light-bulb moment came when I understood that she was really just trying to connect with me and deal with her insecurities. She was seeking my love! This realization prompted a fundamental paradigm shift in my thinking."

He gets it! Using Ephesians 5:33, I explain the Crazy Cycle this way: When a wife feels unloved, she reacts in ways that feel disrespectful to her husband, and when a husband feels disrespected, he reacts in ways that feel unloving to his wife. This dynamic spins, and the relationship can get crazy!

So I point out to every husband that when he sees the spirit of his wife deflate, she is probably feeling unloved. When that happens, he needs to recognize that his wife is reacting defensively because she is feeling unloved. Unfortunately, she ends up offending him with her disrespectful words and actions. Instead of reacting in an unloving manner, he needs to decode that she is saying, "You are the only man in my life who can meet my need for love, and I need to feel your love."

A wife feels strongly that if her husband loves her in his heart, he will communicate that love.

This does not necessarily mean that a husband must shower his wife with romantic poetry daily. But she expects him to somehow, sometime tell her of his love if it is in his heart.

It is no coincidence that early on in the Bible—in describing the first marriage in human history—there is a living definition of the meaning of closeness. "Therefore shall a man leave his father and his mother, and shall cleave unto his wife: and they shall be one flesh" (Genesis 2:24 KJV).

When Scripture speaks of "cleaving," the idea in the Hebrew is to cling, hold, or keep close. Two are joined together face to face, becoming one flesh. Your wife will feel loved when you move toward her and let her know you want to be close with a look, a touch, or a smile.

Connecting is what women look for in any relationship, and especially in marriage. Your wife will feel loved when you move toward her and let her know you want to be close with a look, a touch, or a smile,

One way to picture your marriage is with a line that has the word *Involvement* at one end and the word *Independence* at the other:

Involvement —————————————————————— Independence

Typically, women will lean toward the "Involvement" side while men lean more toward the "Independence" side. But when a man moves toward his wife and shows her he wants to connect in even little ways, this motivates and energizes her.

BEING CLOSE COSTS NOTHING —
BUT YOUR TIME *and* LOVE.

The tension between involvement and independence is another illustration of the difference between pink and blue.

As a man, you will probably not be able to be as involved with your wife as much as she may like. You are a man, and your wife loves you for being a man, not a woman. She doesn't expect you to become feminine, just like her girlfriend. But when you move toward her, when you show her you want to connect in even small ways, watch what happens. This movement will motivate her. It will energize her.

Do you realize the power of just holding your wife's hand?

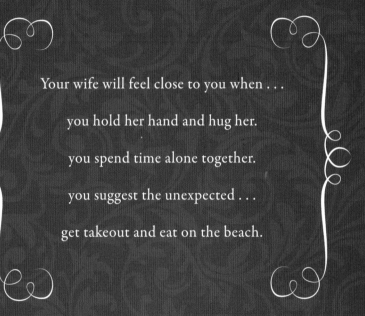

Your wife will feel close to you when . . .

you hold her hand and hug her.

you spend time alone together.

you suggest the unexpected . . .

get takeout and eat on the beach.

If *a* MARITAL CONFLICT EXISTS,
IT AFFECTS *a* WOMAN'S ENTIRE BEING.
WHEN SHE BELIEVES THERE IS *a*
PROBLEM, HER SPIRIT *is* CRUSHED.
THAT'S WHY MOST WIVES PREFER *to*
TALK ABOUT MARITAL PROBLEMS
ON *a* DAILY BASIS *to* KEEP THE
RELATIONSHIP "UP-TO-DATE."
THEY FEEL *that* BEING OPEN LIKE
THIS PREVENTS ANY MAJOR
PROBLEM FROM DEVELOPING.

As the church places her burdens on Christ, so a woman needs to place her burdens on her husband. When she shares with you, don't assume she is asking you to solve her problem.

Ask your wife, "Do you want a solution or a listening ear?"

HOW CAN YOU BE AN UNDERSTANDING HUSBAND?

The most powerful weapons you have are your ears. Just listen to your wife, and she is much more likely to feel understood.

To "just listen" is usually not a husband's strong suit. He is better built to analyze, give answers, and "fix" the situation. The unaware husband doesn't readily decode the messages his wife is sending when she comes to him with her problems.

The truth is, you really don't have to fix her problem; generally all she really wants is your listening ear. As a husband, if you can grasp that you don't always have to solve your wife's problems, you will take a giant step toward showing her empathy and understanding.

You husbands in the same way,
live with your wives in an
understanding way, as with
someone weaker, since she is a woman;
and show her honor as a fellow heir
of the grace of life, so that your
prayers will not be hindered.

–1 PETER 3:7

You show your wife
understanding when . . .

- you don't try to "fix her problems"
  unless she specifically asks for a
  solution.

- you try to identify her feelings.

- you don't interrupt her when she's
  trying to tell you how she feels.

For any husband who wants fewer ongoing arguments, the path to peace is plain. He must learn to simply say, "Honey, I'm sorry. Will you forgive me? I didn't mean to do that."

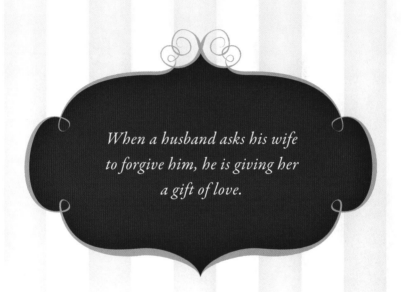

When a husband asks his wife to forgive him, he is giving her a gift of love.

Loyalty spells love to a wife, but if she lacks assurance because her husband's actions or words make her feel even vaguely insecure, she might say things like "Do you really love me? I sometimes wonder"; "Do you want me for me? Sometimes I'm not really sure"; or, perhaps trying to mask her feelings with a joking question, "Tell me. Will you stay with me when I'm old and gray?"

WITH THESE REMARKS SHE *is* NOT TRYING *to* BE DISRESPECTFUL *or* SUGGESTING YOU ARE DISLOYAL. SHE SIMPLY LONGS *to* KNOW THAT ONLY DEATH WILL EVER SEPARATE YOU.

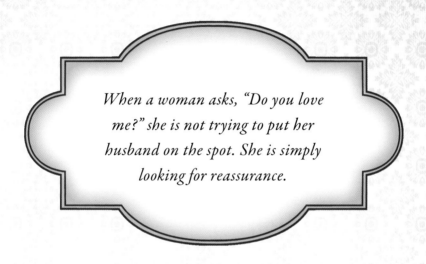

When a woman asks, "Do you love me?" she is not trying to put her husband on the spot. She is simply looking for reassurance.

Your wife is assured of your loyalty
when . . .

you speak highly of her in front of
your children and others.

you don't look lustfully at other women.

you call and let her know your plans.

you keep commitments.

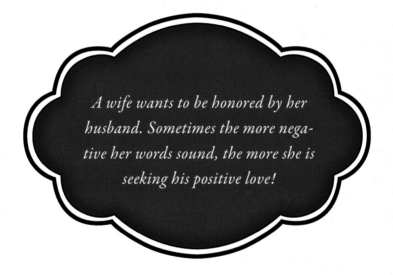

A wife wants to be honored by her husband. Sometimes the more negative her words sound, the more she is seeking his positive love!

A wise husband decodes his wife's negative words; a foolish husband just gets angry and lashes back or goes the other direction and stonewalls her with silence.

If a husband pledges Love and a wife pledges Respect, but they speak words that feel unloving and disrespectful, they simply plant seeds of doubt about what is really in their hearts.

One woman said to her husband, "I just got off the phone with my sister. She's incredible. She tells me that she helped her husband build a back porch on their house this summer. She also made a rocking chair, and she's in an exotic foods cooking class. She's always doing something, making something. I feel so inadequate when I talk with her. What do *I* make?"

Her husband turned to her and said, "You make me happy."

Bingo! Bonus points for that husband! He knows how to esteem his wife.

God has made women so that they
want to be honored and respected.
The way to honor your wife, as well
as to honor your covenant with God,
is to treasure her.

I have heard men who suddenly lost their wives make tearful admissions. One broken widower confessed, "I wish I would have told her how much she meant to me. How can you live so long with a person and not see the treasure in front of your eyes?"

Your wife feels honored when . . .

you give her encouragement or praise.

you are physically affectionate
with her in public.

you choose family outings
over "guy things."

you let her know that you are proud
of her and all she does.

Husband, do you want God's favor?
He favors you when you submit to
your wife's need for love,
understanding, loyalty, and honor!

HE *Needs* RESPECT

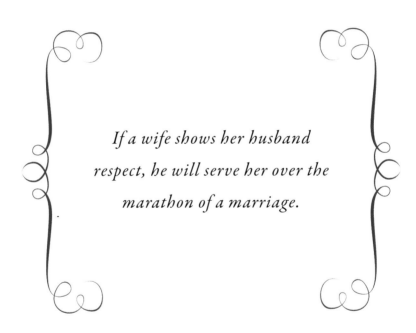

If a wife shows her husband respect, he will serve her over the marathon of a marriage.

Whenever I teach that a man needs respect, I can be sure of hearing this from some women: "Dr. Emerson, I don't feel any respect for my husband. It would be hypocritical for me to show him respect when I don't feel it, and I don't feel respect for him because he does not deserve it. He has not earned respect by loving me in meaningful ways, and everyone knows he must earn respect in order to get respect. Besides, respect is for our superiors, and my husband is not superior to me. I am not inferior to him. We are equals. So I am not going be treated like a doormat and subject myself to emotional abuse. Frankly, this call to respect is all about him, his ego, and his narcissism, and I'm not going to feed his chauvinistic tendencies. I am definitely not going to live in fear of his domination and set the feminist movement back fifty years. But other than that, I'm really open to hearing what you have to say about this."

After listening to these comments, I ask, "Do you have a son?" Then I offer this explanation: If you do have a son, your future daughter-in-law, who does not have a mean bone in her body and is the epitome of sweetness, will have this same he-hasn't-earned-my-respect attitude toward your precious baby boy. Consequently, he will shut down, close off, and withdraw in profound hurt. Then your daughter-in-law will label him unloving—and may even go on a talk show to tell the world!

Many a mouth drops open, and the women exclaim, "That daughter-in-law better not show such disrespect to my baby boy!"

And these women have an awakening. They feel one way about their husbands, and they feel quite differently about their precious baby boys. It hits them that their husbands were once baby boys and if their daughters-in-law treat their sons the way they themselves are treating their husbands, there's a storm on the horizon.

Any man knows that if his wife respects him in her heart, she will communicate that respect.

This does not mean that a wife must compose songs of admiration and sing them to him at sunrise and sunset. But at some time, in some simple way, the message will come through if respect is truly in her heart.

That a husband values respect more than love is very difficult for many women to grasp. God has made you to love, and you see life through pink lenses that are focused on love. You give love, you want love, and you may not quite understand why your husband does not operate the same way. When I say a husband values respect more than love, do I mean that your husband does not value love at all?

OF COURSE HE VALUES *your* LOVE — MORE *than* WORDS CAN DESCRIBE — BUT HE SPELLS LOVE R-E-S-P-E-C-T.

When I say that a husband needs respect, I am not saying that he deserves the respect. I am saying that he needs to be approached respectfully when she confronts the issues about him that upset her just as she needs him to approach her lovingly and respectfully when he addresses the issues about her that concern him.

In order for her husband to hear her heart, a wife must offer him respect. No human being responds to contempt, and no husband feels love and affection in his heart toward a wife he thinks despises all he is as a human being.

He will not move toward her to connect with her; instead he will withdraw and stonewall. A wife's disrespect cannot motivate her husband to be loving. A wife expresses, "I had a light-bulb moment when you told of a letter a woman sent to you saying she acted very disrespectfully in order to send a message to her husband that she felt unloved and that she thought this would motivate him to love her. That is exactly what I do/did, and now I get it! I completely get it."

As a wife, if you can start to understand how important your husband's work is to him, you will take a giant step toward communicating respect and honor, two things that he values even more than your love.

A man has a natural, inborn desire to go out and "conquer" the challenges of his world—to work and achieve.

If a woman criticizes her husband's work in any way, he will feel disrespected *every time she does this*.

The desire to provide for his wife is something God put deep within every man's soul. Admittedly, men are very sensitive to put-downs in this area of providing for the family.

Your husband knows you appreciate his
desire to protect and provide when . . .

you praise his commitment to
provide for you.

you empathize when he reveals his
male mind-set about position, status,
or rank at work.

you never put down his job or how
much he makes.

A man who has basic goodwill will serve his wife and even die for her.

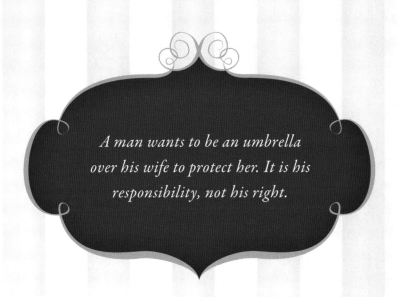

A man wants to be an umbrella over his wife to protect her. It is his responsibility, not his right.

Some people say the Bible puts down women. Actually the Bible holds up women and gives them advice on how to realize their fondest desires.

As a wife, you don't have to fight for your rights. You don't have to push and push and struggle to understand your husband as you try to move closer only to have him coldly move away.

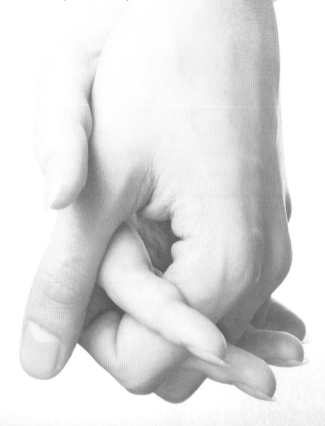

There is another way to get his love, and the Bible tells you what it is. Your quiet and respectful behavior will win him.

THIS *is* THE KEY *to* EMPOWERMENT: YOU GET WHAT YOU WANT BY GIVING HIM WHAT HE WANTS.

It's true that women have intuition and that men should listen to them.

It's also true that women have blind spots and need the insight of their husbands.

In many marriages it is all too easy for a wife to write off a husband's insight and suggestions because she thinks she doesn't need them or he has no right to give them. But I believe husband and wife together need to examine any situation where something is amiss and try to come to a solution or, if needed, seek godly counsel.

Men grow close by doing activities together, shoulder to shoulder. Over time, these common experiences and mutual interests result in a sense of bonding. Many men can recall being a "blood brother" with his boyhood friend. Two drops of blood blended together symbolized the "forever" bond. The commitment was to be shoulder to shoulder, fighting to the death, if need be.

One day, the little boy grows up, becomes a man, and meets a special young woman. He proposes, and they marry. In his maleness, he assumes the two of them will be together, shoulder to shoulder, just as he has been with his male friends throughout his life. His request is simple: "Hey, let's go do something together."

The wife who wants to show her husband that she likes him—that she is his friend—will be patient with his strange request to "just come out here and be with me. Watch what I am doing, or just watch TV with me, but let's not talk." When the husband calls the wife in to "just sit by him," he is working on their relationship in a significant way—not significant to her, perhaps, but extremely significant, nonetheless. This is the way a husband communicates.

FROM *a* MAN'S PERSPECTIVE. . . .
ENJOYING TIME TOGETHER
DOESN'T ALWAYS INCLUDE DEEP,
MEANINGFUL CONVERSATION.

You show appreciation for your
husband's insight when . . .

you thank him for his advice
without acting insulted.

you let him "fix things" and
applaud his solutions.

you thank him for his perception
and godly counsel.

Men are solution oriented.
They love to solve problems.
They want to be helpful.

When a wife is friendly and shows that she likes her husband, particularly by doing shoulder-to-shoulder activities with him, he will feel respected. But when she becomes so immersed in her own schedule and duties she seems to have no time for him, then she might hear something like "Can't you let that go for a few minutes?" A wife could respond to this request with "Don't you know I have a lot to do?" or she can decode her husband's message, put her duties on hold for a little while, and say, "Sure, watching with you will be fun."

THE KEY, HOWEVER, IS *to* RESPOND
IN *a* TRULY FRIENDLY WAY,
NOT RESIGNEDLY LIKE *a* MARTYR
OR IN *the* SLIGHTEST WAY
BEGRUDGINGLY.

Being friendly to her man is one of the most effective things a woman can do to strengthen her marriage.

Your husband knows you value
his friendship when . . .

you tell him you like him and you show
it (he knows you love him, but he often
wonders if you really like him).

you do recreational activities together,

you encourage him to open up and talk
to you as you do things
shoulder to shoulder.

COMMUNICATING LOVE AND RESPECT

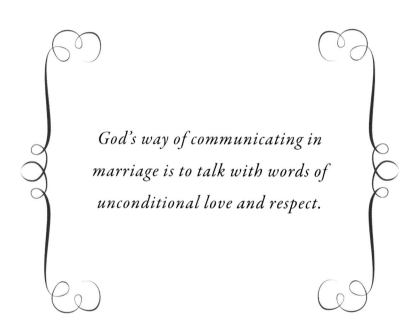

God's way of communicating in marriage is to talk with words of unconditional love and respect.

"If," comments a wife, "I'm in the middle of a conversation with my husband that has the potential to become heated and a negative thought about my husband enters my mind, I remember the simple advice in Love and Respect that when I communicate with my husband, I need respectful words, a respectful tone of voice, and a respectful countenance. I also remember the simple advice that I need to think respectful thoughts about my husband because he is created in the image of God, and God commands me to respect him."

I also teach "my response is my responsibility." When my spouse and I get on the Crazy Cycle, my unloving words are my responsibility. My wife, Sarah, doesn't cause my unloving words, and I must always ask myself before I speak, "Is that which I am about to say going to sound loving or unloving to Sarah?"

A husband comments, "Our relationship changed from frequent nagging and fighting when I realized that my response is my responsibility. I find myself constantly going back to that [truth] in every situation that gets heated. Our relationship has gradually gotten better and better as I try to speak lovingly."

It would be easy enough to deduce that communication is the key to marriage, but I don't agree. To say that communication is the key to marriage is to assume that both spouses speak the same language.

After more than three decades of pastoring, counseling married couples, and conducting marriage conferences, I have learned that, in fact, the wife speaks a "love language" and the husband speaks a "respect language." They don't realize this, of course, but because he is speaking one kind of language (respect) and she is speaking another (love), there is little or no understanding and little or no communication.

Your words are a very good indication of what is going on in your heart—and your spouse knows it.

Just about every couple knows what it is like to get into a conflict that escalates into a full-blown argument and they are not sure why it happened. Spouses tend to write off these kinds of arguments, saying, "If only she weren't so sensitive" or "If only he weren't so touchy." But those aren't the real issues at all.

Conflict inevitably happens when spouses focus on their own needs and overlook the needs of the other. That's when the issues arise. The wife needs love; she is not trying to be disrespectful. The husband needs respect; he is not trying to be unloving. And once the Love and Respect couple grasps a basic principle—that the apparent issue is not the real issue at all—they are on their way to cracking the communication code.

The heart of the wise instructs
his mouth
And adds persuasiveness to his lips.

—PROVERBS 16:23

Conflict is inevitable;
it is simply part of living together.

The key to keeping conflict from escalating is to choose to practice love or respect. When a husband speaks with a loving tone during a conflict, which may range from a mild argument to a more serious disagreement, his wife will feel one with him. And when a wife softens her facial expressions and comes across more respectfully during those times of friction, the husband will feel one with her.

Will the disagreement be solved? Perhaps, but more than likely it will still be there. Yet husband and wife can feel oneness because nobody has to win and nobody has to lose. Winning or losing during conflict is not the goal. Oneness is, and it is gained when the wife feels loved by her husband and the husband feels respected by his wife. They bond with each other; two, indeed, become one.

No matter what your struggle—
criticism, constant conflict, sex,
money, parenting, harsh words—
learning to communicate the Love
and Respect way can help you make
crucial changes and build the kind
of relationship that God blesses.

My first *and* most important rule for better everyday communication *is* simply Take time *to* be clear.

And *to* be clear, speak carefully *to* be understood.

And, just as important, listen carefully *to* understand.

This rule is easy to say, but not always easy to remember to do. It is all too easy to mind read or jump to conclusions, and sometimes you can just be plain lazy in expressing yourself, assuming your partner will know what you mean. But your spouse doesn't always know what you mean, and the possibilities of a tiny misunderstanding growing into something a lot more serious are legion.

IT'S CRUCIAL *to* COMMUNICATE WITH THE RIGHT TONE *of* VOICE AND THE RIGHT EXPRESSION *on* YOUR FACE.

This is a problem for men and women, but for different reasons. I have counseled many couples where the wife complains that the husband comes across as harsh and unloving. From her pink perspective, he is frowning with disapproval or sounding stern, even angry. According to his blue point of view, he is simply making his point firmly and accurately. Obviously, he needs to put on his wife's pink sunglasses and pink hearing aids and see how he really looks and sounds to her. A guy can be oblivious to the damaging effects of his angry glare.

At the same time I've had many wives tell me they know they are guilty of a negative tone of voice and a sour look on their faces. They don't necessarily sound harsh; theirs is more a tone of contempt, often accompanied by a rolling of the eyes. The pink wife who is guilty of this kind of behavior needs to put on her husband's blue sunglasses and blue hearing aids so she can realize how disrespectfully she is coming across to him.

These three proverbs provide thought-provoking word pictures about what it means to speak and listen carefully:

Proverbs 18:13—"He who gives an answer before he hears, it is folly and shame to him."

Proverbs 15:28—"The heart of the righteous ponders how to answer, but the mouth of the wicked pours out evil things."

Proverbs 16:23—"The heart of the wise instructs his mouth and adds persuasiveness to his lips."

If you listen before you answer . . .
if you think before you speak . . .
if your heart instructs your mouth . . .
then what you say will make your
wife feel loved or your husband feel
respected.

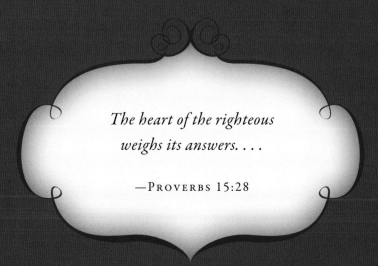

The heart of the righteous
weighs its answers. . . .

—Proverbs 15:28

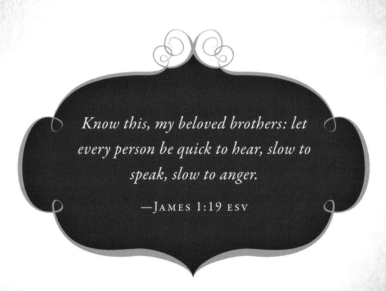

Know this, my beloved brothers: let every person be quick to hear, slow to speak, slow to anger.

—James 1:19 esv

Marital researchers agree that a huge percentage of communication problems between husband and wife are due not to what is said but to how it is said—the attitude and tone of voice.

Despite your best intentions, minor breakdowns or glitches in communication do occur. When they happen, don't accuse your spouse of not listening carefully or speaking clearly. Instead, make your own move to clarify things. If your spouse seems unclear, say, "I'm sorry. I guess I didn't understand. What I thought you said was . . . [Then state what you heard as best you can.] Is that correct?"

Or, if it is apparent that your spouse either did not hear you correctly or has misinterpreted your words, say, "I'm sorry. I was not as clear as I could have been. What I meant to say was . . . [Then restate what you are trying to convey as best you can.] Is that what you heard me saying?"

Many women believe that if they remain quiet and don't share their feelings as much as they think is necessary, they will lose their power and sense of self, nothing will ever be resolved in their marriage, and no improvement will ever happen. The wife who has these fears should remember that God's instructions always have a profound purpose. From what we hear at Love and Respect Conferences and by e-mail, many husbands are convicted and motivated to change far more quickly when a wife comes across respectfully with a gentle and quiet spirit.

My word of encouragement to all wives married to a good-willed man is this: as you practice quietness and unconditional respect, your marriage will improve, issues will get resolved, and your sense of self and power will increase.

*Your adornment must not be
merely external—braiding the
hair, and wearing gold jewelry, or
putting on dresses; but let it be the
hidden person of the heart, with
the imperishable quality of a gentle
and quiet spirit, which is precious
in the sight of God.*

—1 PETER 6:3–4

The good-willed husband who is willing to work at listening better must remember he will face obstacles, and one of the most intriguing that he should be ready to deal with is spiderwebbing.

Spiderwebbing happens when someone starts with this point and goes to that point but doesn't finish that point before going on to another point. Multitasking women are masters of this art, but the average husband is totally confused by it because God designed him to be linear. He is wired to finish one point completely and then move on to the next. When he gets together with his wife and she starts bouncing from one point to another—fully intending to come back and finish each point—he gets that blank, faraway look in his eyes.

So what's the answer? Should women try to totally give up spiderwebbing and become linear thinkers and talkers? That's not likely to happen this side of the Promised Land. So what couples must do is give each other a measure of grace. Husbands need to let their wives release their emotions and share their reports. Wives need to do this with as little spiderwebbing as possible, saving the longer versions for girlfriends.

A *Love* and
RESPECT THAT LASTS

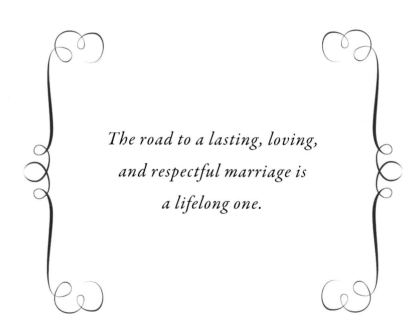

The road to a lasting, loving, and respectful marriage is a lifelong one.

Did you know that even if we are married to an unresponsive spouse we can still show love and respect to him or her as "unto Christ"? Believers in Christ need this reminder: at the end of life, we will stand before Christ and He will evaluate how we treated Him based on how we treated our spouse. In principle, we are to apply in our marriage the principle Jesus taught in Matthew 25:40—"Truly I say to you, to the extent that you did it to one of these brothers of Mine, even the least of them, you did it to Me." The apostle Paul applies this teaching specifically to husbands and wives (Ephesians 5:22, 25).

"I had fallen short of loving my wife as Christ loves the church," a husband shares. "I was not living my marriage as unto the Lord. I then realized that it's not about my wife and me having differences, but it's about me living for Christ." Similarly, a wife says, "I have skipped the part about my husband showing love to me because, quite frankly, it doesn't matter. I have resolved to do the right thing as unto Jesus Christ and then let the chips fall where they may. I have to say that it has not been easy. It is a discipline and a choice."

The truth is, it is easier for many a man to die for honor than to move toward a contemptuous wife in a loving way, saying, "I believe I was wrong. Can we talk about this?" To turn to your wife in the middle of a conflict and say, "I am sorry. Will you forgive me?" takes guts. It isn't pleasant, but it works powerfully. Over time it becomes easier, but it is never natural. Even so, this response gives you the power to drain the negativity out of your wife in conflict after conflict.

AND THE BEST PART OF *it* IS THAT YOU, *the* MALE WHO TENDS *to* SEE AND HEAR LIFE THROUGH BLUE, WILL TOUCH YOUR PINK WIFE IN THE TENDER *and* LOVING WAY SHE DESIRES.

To the world it may make no sense
for a wife to put on respect toward a
husband who is harsh and unloving.
It makes no sense for a husband to
put on love toward a contemptuous,
disrespectful woman. But it makes
sense to God. These seemingly
fruitless efforts matter to God because
this is the kind of service He rewards.
What is wisdom to God is foolishness
to the world (1 Corinthians 3:19).

When you look to God and His Word
as your ultimate source of significance
and security, you don't demand that
your spouse take that role in your life.
And as you draw strength from the
Lord individually, He draws you
closer together as a couple.

Proverbs 24:16 says, "A righteous man falls seven times, and rises again." Nobody can love perfectly and no one can respect perfectly. However, when we do this as unto Christ, we may fall but we can get up.

The difference between successful couples and unsuccessful couples is that the successful ones keep getting up and keep dealing with the issues.

No matter how difficult your spouse may be at the moment, your spouse does not have control over your reaction; you do. You may be experiencing disappointment, frustration, or anger, but you always have a choice.

Marriage is a test of how you unconditionally love and respect your spouse as you obey, honor, and please the Lord. *Primarily*, you don't practice love and respect to meet your needs in your marriage, as important as these are. Your first goal is to obey and please Christ. When you try to do this, often (but not always) your needs are met, and these are wonderful by-products and blessings. But your first goal is to obey and please the Lord.

The road to a lasting Love and Respect marriage is a lifelong one, and there is no way you can travel it in your own strength. The task is overwhelming, and you need help from your heavenly Father, who knows your heart. If you want to do your marriage as unto Christ, you must ask Christ for help.

Let the words of my mouth and the

meditation of my heart

Be acceptable in Your sight,

O Lord, my rock and my Redeemer.

—PSALM 19:14

ONE DEFINITION OF *a* BLESSING IS GIVING PEOPLE SOMETHING *for* WHICH THEY CAN FEEL THANKFUL, SOMETHING *that* MAKES THEM FEEL SECURE, SUPPORTED, CONTENT, *or* ENCOURAGED.

In other words, we can bless our spouses when we are loving or respectful enough to decode their remarks that sound like we have a Love or Respect issue going. Or we can bless our spouses by being loving or respectful enough to clarify something that is unclear to one or both of us.

Our words will either bless or not bless our spouse. That is the time to ask ourselves, "Is what I'm about to say going to result in my spouse feeling loved or unloved? Respected or disrespected?" In either situation, we can be sure the Lord hears! Our words do not escape His notice because we are speaking lovingly or respectfully first for Him and then for our spouse. And as we speak to our husband or wife as unto the Lord, our spouse will be influenced, encouraged, and certainly blessed.

Positive changes flood a relationship immediately when both husband and wife cancel the blame game!

In the ultimate sense,
your marriage has nothing to do with
your spouse. It has everything to do with
your relationship to Jesus Christ.

Wives, be subject to your own husbands,
as to the Lord.—Ephesians 5:22

Husbands, love your wives, just as Christ
also loved the church and gave Himself
up for her.—Ephesians 5:25

When your spouse deflates before your eyes, instead of just defending yourself by saying, "That's your problem," admit that it's *always* also *your* problem. Instead of allowing the conflict to get out of control, you must seek to stop it.

Take your time answering any heated remarks. Think to yourself, *Something is bothering him/her. Instead of getting defensive, I need to go slow, giving him/her the benefit of the doubt. I need to be patient.*

I realized the section on marriage in Ephesians 5:22–5:33 did not address communication between husband and wife. Then it hit me: every text has its larger context. I asked, "What did Paul say earlier about 'talking' which he assumed couples would apply?" Whamo! I discovered five foundational truths about communication:

Words of Love or Respect must be
TRUTHFUL because lies and half-truths
will undermine your relationship.

Words of Love or Respect must UPLIFT your spouse,
edifying—and never manipulating—him or her.

Words of Love or Respect must
include FORGIVENESS because your
spouse is bound to fail you.

Words of Love or Respect must include
THANKFULNESS spoken to or about your spouse;
don't fixate on weaknesses and faults.

Words of Love or Respect must be based and
focused on SCRIPTURE; avoid ideas that are
contrary to the heart of Christ.

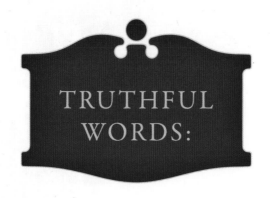

TRUTHFUL WORDS:

ALWAYS SPEAK THE TRUTH, SINCE THE
SMALLEST OF LIES DISCREDITS YOUR
WORDS OF LOVE OR RESPECT.

Laying aside falsehood, speak truth.
(Ephesians 4:25)

Truthful words must be handled with care: a husband or wife is not to speak truth in an unloving or disrespectful way. To say things that just lay your spouse out and then explain, "I was only trying to be honest" can be cruel and deceptive. I know of one husband who finally realized he would use the truth in such a way that he was clubbing people with it, including his wife. He cut way back on his "I'm just being honest" remarks because he realized how unloving he sounded.

UPLIFTING
WORDS:

ALWAYS SPEAK IN AN UPLIFTING WAY
FOR YOUR SPOUSE'S SAKE, AND DO NOT
USE LOVE OR RESPECT AS A
MANIPULATIVE PLOY TO MEET YOUR
OWN NEED FOR LOVE OR RESPECT.

*Let no unwholesome word proceed from
your mouth, but only such a word as is
good for edification. (Ephesians 4:29)*

The NIV translation uses a simpler term for "edification," saying "only what is helpful for building others up."

In a marriage that is functioning with any Love and Respect at all, both spouses speak upliftingly, with gracious words for each other. In so doing they emulate another way that Jesus talked. As Luke points out, "all were speaking well of Him, and wondering at the gracious words which were falling from His lips" (Luke 4:22).

FORGIVING WORDS:

Knowing my spouse will not be able to love or respect me perfectly, I commit to having a forgiving spirit so that I may never speak hatefully or contemptuously.

Let all bitterness and wrath and anger . . .
and slander be put away from you, along
with all malice . . . And be . . . forgiving . . .
just as God in Christ has forgiven you.
(Ephesians 4:31–32)

When you possess a forgiving spirit, words of Love or Respect will flow authentically from your lips—and realize that the Lord Himself is listening to you at moments like these. He knows you are not powerless, but actually full of power that He has granted you. He knows you are not weak, foolish, or afraid, wanting peace at any price. Instead He sees you as godly and wise, committed to imitating Him, and longing to hear His "Well done!"

Forgiving my mate is the way I learned Christ. Jesus forgave me therefore I will forgive my spouse.

THANKFUL
WORDS:

SINCE IT IS EASY TO BE NEGATIVE,
FOCUS ON YOUR MATE'S GOOD
QUALITIES AND EXPRESS THANKS
WITH POSITIVE WORDS OF LOVE
OR RESPECT.

There must be no filthiness and silly talk,
or coarse jesting, which are not fitting,
but rather giving of thanks.
(Ephesians 5:4)

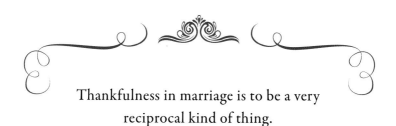

Thankfulness in marriage is to be a very reciprocal kind of thing.

If you want your husband to express appreciation for your attempts to be respectful, you must speak thankfully when he tries to be loving.

If you want your wife to express appreciation for your attempts to be loving, you must use Thankful Words when she tries to speak or act respectfully.

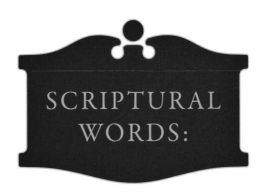

SCRIPTURAL WORDS:

To stay the course in speaking words of Love or Respect, keep your heart in Scripture, trusting in and talking about His promises to help you.

Speaking to one another in psalms and hymns and spiritual songs . . . making melody with your heart to the Lord.
(Ephesians 5:19)

Speaking Scriptural Words does
not mean that you must quote the Bible
every time you open your mouth,
but it does mean that you are thinking
about God's promises and trusting Him.
Speaking Scriptural Words is living
and talking according to God's
principles and values.

Four keys to a God-ordained marriage:

1. When one of you makes a mistake, control any anger you may feel and trust God completely no matter what happens.

2. Depend on God, not your mate, to meet all your needs.

3. Trust God when the "why's" of life threaten to overwhelm you.

4. Remember that life is not first about the two of you and your marriage. It's first about your commitment to Jesus Christ and doing everything you do for Him.

No one can really practice Love and
Respect unless he or she does it as
unto Jesus Christ.

If you and your spouse are not taking time to pray together, I urge you to do so. Prayer can be a tremendous opportunity for the husband in particular as he invites his wife to talk to the Lord about whatever is concerning them. One thing is for sure: there is power when two people pray. For example, God may be allowing the two of you to have a problem because His deepest purpose is that the two of you come together and find wisdom and strength in Him.

You need only spend *a* few minutes expressing *to* God the concerns *of* your heart. Yet I know some men feel praying with their wives *is* unmanly. On the contrary, if your wife *is* typical, she will see you as more of *a* man because she wants you *to* be the family's spiritual leader. She feels more secure when you take *an* active role in guiding Bible reading *and* praying together.

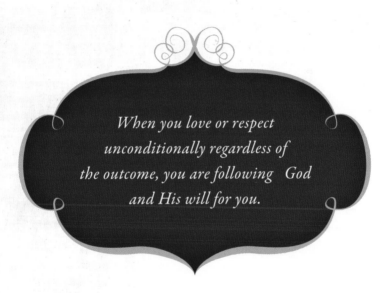

When you love or respect
unconditionally regardless of
the outcome, you are following God
and His will for you.

Sarah and I invite you to visit loveandrespect.com for more information about our Love and Respect resources. We are delighted to serve you with these additional tools. Also, please join our facebook family at facebook.com/loveandrespectministries .

Also Available from this Best-Selling Author,

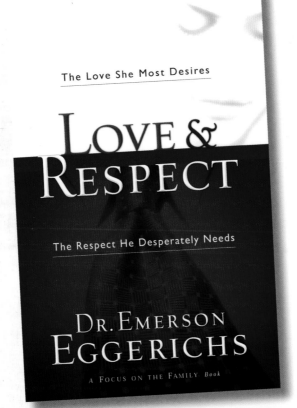

The Love She Most Desires

LOVE & RESPECT

The Respect He Desperately Needs

DR. EMERSON EGGERICHS

A FOCUS ON THE FAMILY *Book*

LOVE & RESPECT
The Love She Most Desires • *The Respect He Desperately Needs*
ISBN: 978-1-59145-187-7

Dr. Emerson Eggerichs

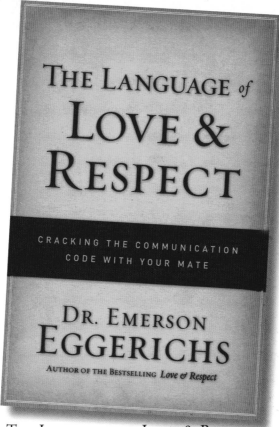

THE LANGUAGE OF LOVE & RESPECT
A Revolutionary Solution to the #1 Marriage Problem
ISBN: 978-0-8499-4807-7